All About Data

Charmaine Robertson

Rosen REAL READERS

Rosen Classroom™
New York

I am doing a project.

It is about paper planes.

Which kind of plane flies best?
My teacher says I need data.

Data is a collection of facts.
I find data in books.

I find data online.

I use a computer.

My teacher helps me.

I write down what I find.

I learn a lot about paper planes.

Words to Know

books

computer

paper planes

write